Kowtow!

About the Author

WILLIAM SHAWCROSS is a writer and journalist. His books include *Dubcek, Sideshow: Kissinger, Nixon and the Destruction of Cambodia, The Quality of Mercy: Cambodia, Holocaust and Modern Conscience*, and *The Shah's Last Ride: The Story of the Exile, Misadventures and Death of The Emperor*. He is now writing a book about Rupert Murdoch and the communications revolution.

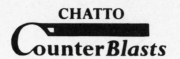
CHATTO
C **ounter** ***Blasts***

William
SHAWCROSS

Kowtow!

Chatto & Windus
LONDON

Published in 1989 by
Chatto & Windus Ltd
30 Bedford Square
London WC1B 3SG

A CIP catalogue record for this book
is available from the British Library

ISBN 0 7011 3628 6

Photoset in Linotron Ehrhardt by
Rowland Phototypesetting Ltd
Bury St Edmunds, Suffolk
Printed in Great Britain by
St Edmundsbury Press Ltd
Bury St Edmunds, Suffolk

I hear the call of democracy, it is ringing in my
    mind;
I can feel the sparks of freedom, they are burning
    in my heart.
Like our thinkers of the past who dared to dream,
I must follow in their steps.
I, too, am prepared to bleed,
and I will give my life, as they did,
for this, our beloved land.

The past is over. After five thousand years of
    feudalism,
we must break our chains.
The past is finished. After forty years of tyranny,
we must abandon our chains.
For this, I have become a willing seed . . .

Goodby forever,
my mother,
my country.

4 May 1989 Tiananmen Square

This poem was written by a fifteen-year-old boy
and sent to his family one month before his death
in Tiananmen Square. After the massacre, it was
posted on the Cenotaph in Hong Kong.

'PRIME MINISTER, on Wednesday you signed an agreement with China promising to deliver over five million people into the hands of a communist dictatorship. Is this morally defensible, or is it really true that in international politics the highest form of morality is one's own national interests?'

This question was put to Mrs Thatcher in December 1984 when she visited Hong Kong to praise the agreement she had just signed with China on handing Hong Kong back to Peking in 1997. The questioner was Emily Lau of the *Far Eastern Economic Review*. Mrs Thatcher was evidently displeased. In her reply, she asked what would have happened had there been no agreement on preserving Hong Kong's lifestyle. 'I think you would have had great cause to complain had the government of Great Britain done nothing until 1997 and I believe that most of the people in Hong Kong think the same. You may be the solitary exception.'

Mrs Thatcher's infelicitous riposte was inappropriate then. But people hoped. Today, almost five years later, the solitary exceptions have become the overwhelming majority of the people of Hong Kong.

Because of British pusillanimity. And because of the massacre.

On the night of 3–4 June 1989, Chinese tanks and troops slaughtered hundreds if not thousands of people, many of them students who had been peacefully demonstrating for democracy in Tiananmen Square in the centre of Peking. The broken bodies of young people lay tangled and mangled with their broken bicycles.

The massacre aroused a spontaneous overflow of powerful feelings around the world. Indeed, I believe that it is an event which will and should change international and individual views in the same way as did the invasions of Hungary and Czechoslovakia. No longer can China be given the benefit of international doubt, a benefit which it has used so skilfully in the last two decades.

Nowhere has the impact of the massacre been greater than in Hong Kong, where it literally caused terror – precisely because of Britain's agreement to hand the Crown Colony over to China in 1997. But while the panic of British citizens in Hong Kong grew, British ministers and their Labour Party counterparts acted in rare unison, mouthing unctuous platitudes as they busily softsoaped Hong Kong and tried to look away from Tiananmen. As they denied that Britain could offer haven to its own citizens, it seemed to me as if the last act of empire would be its most discreditable and disastrous.

We are talking about the future of almost six million people, in the Age of the Refugee. There are now at least twelve million refugees in the world, including 45,000 Vietnamese boat people who have fled to Hong Kong. The horrifying danger now is that thousands of boats will be leaving Hong Kong at the end of the 1990s.

Remember the spring of 1989. There were a few weeks in April and May when it seemed that half the world was shaking off its chains. Old orders were crumbling and brave new people and ideas were taking charge. Thanks largely to Mikhail Gorbachev, communist dictatorships were being swept away in both Poland and Hungary and his magnificently bold reforms were allowing unprecedented freedoms in the Soviet Union as well.

In China too the changes seemed startling. In the weeks before the massacre the democracy move-ment engendered enormous international sym-pathy. There on the vast tarred parade ground, which the communists had, long ago and wantonly,

3

carved out of old Peking in order to stage the huge, dragooned, repetitive and self-indulgent celebrations of their own power, teenagers and young people now gathered spontaneously in hundreds of thousands to protest. Do you remember the tents and the flags fluttering defiantly in the breeze before the huge icon of Mao? It looked as if the place had been occupied by a foreign army. And so it had. By an army quite alien to the ancient governors of today's China. The troops were from another generation – children who were there to denounce the crimes of their teachers and their government, and to ask, in the most peaceful way, for democracy. There was something extraordinarily poignant and optimistic in the fact that after forty years of being force-fed Maoist liturgy, the symbol the students built in the square should be a version of the Statue of Liberty – their own Goddess of Democracy.

For over a month the government adopted the same non-violent tactics as the students. The occupation of Tiananmen was allowed even to disrupt the historic visit of Mikhail Gorbachev, who had come to rebuild Sino-Soviet relations after a split of thirty years. For a time, it seemed as if this beautiful, peaceful protest would succeed. The hope was that, in their anxiety to modernise China by linking its economy to the modern world, Peking would forswear the brutality which almost all dictatorships have used to destroy dissent. May 1989

4

was a time of great expectations. Until the Fourth of June.

This, I believe, was the first massacre seen live or almost at once on television screens around the world. I saw it in New York all that Sunday, 5 June, together with a young Chinese couple studying in America. They were in tears as they watched replay after replay of the tanks rolling over the tents of their friends in the dark and flaming corners of central Peking. At once the slaughter in the streets around Tiananmen became a product of what is called the Information Revolution – the linking, but perhaps not the binding, of the world by satellite and by other fine new technologies such as the Personal Computer and the Fax. Indeed, this could be called the Fax Revolution, for all through May and June students and their supporters around the world evaded censorship by faxing information to and from each other, in and out of China. It is impossible to overemphasise the subversive power of the Fax. In Czechoslovakia after the 1968 invasion, I smuggled documents in and out of the country in my socks or the seats of my car. These days they can be zapped down the phone line in secret seconds. For dissidents everywhere the Fax will become an invaluable, powerful tool.

There are those who declare that this Information Revolution will liberate absolutely. Its repercussions are only just beginning. But certainly the impact of technology was in this case all on the side of the oppressed. Consider another, unseen and unsung, massacre. Who is even aware of the fact that in 1982 the Syrian régime murdered 25,000 of its people in the town of Hama, over one weekend, in bloody silence and to no protest? By contrast, the effect of the instant pictures and testimony from Tiananmen was at once enormous and continues as this pamphlet is being written. But my subject is Hong Kong.

In Hong Kong the massacre created panic – and a sense of betrayal. There the Chinese democracy movement was followed with passion: thousands of people, students and others, assisted in it. They sent money, supporters, tents, sleeping bags, walkie-talkies, more money and, of course, faxed messages to Peking – all in the hope that the movement would at last create a China, a homeland, into which the Hong Kong Chinese could calmly be absorbed by 1997.

Both before and after the massacre, vast and unprecedented crowds of over a million people took to the streets of Hong Kong. They were at first euphoric and proud, and then outraged, grieving and frightened. They pasted poems and exhortations on the cenotaph in Statue Square in Central,

6

the business district of Hong Kong. It was as if the city state had suddenly been awakened from its apolitical slumber – but, alas, by a toad not a prince. People saw the future and recoiled.

You would not guess it by listening now to either the British government or to leaders of the Labour opposition. But the British handover of Hong Kong in 1997 will be an event unique not only in the history of the British Empire, but also of the modern world. For a simple reason, to do with what we call freedom.

The age of decolonisation has created scores of new countries over the last thirty years. By no means all of these countries now enjoy freedom, but all were given independence. Hong Kong will be given neither. Some six million people who now possess most basic freedoms – of the press, of assembly, of protest, but critically not of representation – will be handed over to a dictatorship where no such freedoms exist, and where the demand for them can be crushed by tanks.

The massacre in Tiananmen means this: unless there is a radical change in China, Hong Kong cannot be handed over either with hope or even with what many British officials have possessed in abundance, wishful thinking. The people of Hong Kong no longer have to fear the unknown on 1 July 1997. Now it is the known which terrifies.

After the massacre of the children of Peking

7

came the massacre of the truth. That was, if anything, even more frightening for Hong Kong – and for the rest of the world. Peking has embarked upon the most monstrous but skilful lies about the massacre. Night after night now, precise but unscrupulously recut film is shown to China's five hundred million viewers to demonstrate the kind heroism of the People's Liberation Army. Gone are the tanks roaring over the tents in the night. Vanished entirely is the wonderful image of the lone young man who stood against a column of tanks. Instead we have endless pictures of soldiers sweeping streets, shaking hands with old ladies, cuddling children. Now only a few tears in the tarmac, bullet scars in the fabric, remain as witnesses to 4 June. The lie has been so total, so pervasive, that even some of those who saw the protest and then the massacre themselves might well have begun to question their memories. What of the multitude of Chinese whose knowledge comes only from the government screen in every village? Well, probably they know full well that a lie is a lie is a lie, especially when told by their government.

Meanwhile, young men have been frogmarched, broken, into courts where judges in military apparel have ordered their judicial murder for their parts in the 'counter-revolution'. (Deng Xiao Ping himself has stressed that execution is 'an indispensable tool of political education'.) Thousands of other people have been harried and arrested – in all of China, it seems, there is no attic in which to hide: the fear is so great. Some student leaders have been turned in by their own families – as pretty a demonstration as any of the society which China is today. Lucky ones have escaped surreptitiously through Hong Kong. Peking is now constantly denouncing Hong Kong, and individuals within it, for aiding and abetting the protests, and has warned that if this continues Hong Kong will not know a moment's peace. All this, and much, much more, has sowed terror in the colony.

Now, after the massacre, people have had to accept what they were hoping was no longer true – that rationality is not as important to the Chinese leaders as survival, or as power. The fear of chaos, often cited as overwhelming among Chinese statesmen, allowed them to commit grossly irrational (as well as brutal) acts which seem utterly against China's national interest. The only rational explanation of the massacre and its aftermath is also discouraging: in the last resort the Middle Kingdom, ancient, introverted China, is more important to the Peking leaders than an outward-looking state, coupled to a thriving Hong Kong.

After the massacre many individuals in Hong Kong, and pressure groups, new and old, issued demands. For democracy; for a Bill of Rights;

9

for a tougher line in talks with China now; for international monitoring of China's behaviour after 1997. But first of all, the British citizens of Hong Kong begged Britain, Hong Kong's foster parent, to give them a means of escape – the right of abode in Britain, like other British citizens. And Britain said No.

◇

The massacre created a panic in Westminster too. It was not of the same type as the panic in Hong Kong itself. By contrast, it was contemptible. It was a terror that somehow Britain might become liable for its citizens at the other end of the world. More than 3.28 million people in Hong Kong are entitled to hold British passports, and their spokesmen were demanding the right to live in Britain! The rest of the population is a British responsibility too. There was a bipartisan horror at the thought that obligations of empire would, at this eleventh hour, have to be assumed. When all seemed to be proceeding so quietly and smoothly towards the beginning of the tunnel.

Immediately the Foreign Secretary, Sir Geoffrey Howe, came forward to repeat that it was absolutely out of the question for the Hong Kong Chinese to have the right of abode in Britain. This would do nothing for them, he declared. Back in the 1970s, as one of Mrs Thatcher's voices in the wilderness, Mr Howe used to invoke 'the spirit of Hong Kong' as being just what Britain needed to get its economy going. Later he became the proud British godfather of the agreement on the 1997 handover to China. Sir Geoffrey once compared Hong Kong to a precious Ming vase which had to be passed on in the great relay race of mankind; he was clearly distraught at the idea that his own diplomacy might lead to the smashing of a such an objet d'art. His favourite reason for excluding people now was that 'Parliament would never allow it'. Spokesmen from the Labour Party, the party which proclaims internationalism and the rights of man, rushed to agree. In fact, opinion polls did not show an overwhelming British opposition to the right of abode being granted to the Hong Kong Chinese. People seemed to be divided about fifty-fifty, often even within themselves – thinking that the problems would be immense, but that we should honour our obligation. Yet the Government refused either to listen or to take any lead in forming opinion.

Since her 1984 riposte to Emily Lau, Mrs Thatcher herself has been strangely silent on the subject of Hong Kong. Perhaps she has always sensed inexorable disaster. At question time on 6 June, just two days after the massacre, she ridiculed the idea that the problems of the people of Hong Kong would be resolved by giving them the right of abode in Britain. But her argument had rather more to do with Britain than Hong Kong. She compared the 3.28 million British passport holders in Hong Kong with the 1.6 million 'new Commonwealth' citizens who had come to Britain since 1945. For 'new' read black or brown.

Gerald Kaufman, the Labour spokesman on foreign affairs, condemned the 'abominable' massacres and declared that 'Those of us who have great feelings of friendship for China and have watched its political and economic progress with hope and satisfaction are particularly appalled at this regression to barbarity'. (One wonders whether those more sceptical of Chinese communism might not have been equally appalled.) Kaufman said he supported the refusal to grant right of abode. Later, in a rare display of affection for the Thatcher government, he praised its policy towards Hong Kong. 'I wouldn't do more. I might even do less.' No one else in the Labour leadership had anything better to offer.

The only senior politician to argue for right of abode was Paddy Ashdown, leader of the Social and Liberal Democrats. Mrs Thatcher dismissed his position 'because you have no responsibility whatsoever.' 'Dishonourable', shouted Ashdown, and was compelled to withdraw.

A new word crept into the vocabulary of the crisis – 'flexibility'. This meant that the Government would allow a few more exceptions to the blanket refusal to creep under the wire. There could hardly be less. Till now only seven out of thousands of those applying under the exceptional provisions to come from Hong Kong had been allowed into Britain. Mrs Thatcher agreed that it might be possible to apply the provisions more 'flexibly'. But there was, she said, a world of difference between that 'and saying that 3.5 million people should have right of abode'.

This promise of flexibility was the ultimate weasel word. It meant in effect that we have no plans at this time of honouring any commitment, moral or otherwise, that we might have, but we have no intention of telling *you* that. It meant also that just a few selected civil servants and businessmen would be given coded numbers on a secret list of favoured people to be allowed to slip out of the side door and into Britain, as long as in the meantime they kept the ship afloat, the store open, the writing off the wall. The rest would remain, in the words of the *Independent*, to be handed over, as arranged, 'to whatever group of gentlemen, statesmen, madmen or butchers happens to be ruling China in 1997.'

There was another proposal which was equally outrageous. This was known as the 'Armageddon Scenario'. Sir Geoffrey and other officials promised that if the worst came to the worst, and there was an 'Armageddon' after the Chinese takeover, then

13

of course Britain would have a responsibility to people in Hong Kong. Perhaps this meant that if the British in Hong Kong started fleeing in boats, as the Vietnamese are still doing, they would be picked up – for a time, and until the rest of the world became bored with their endless whining about conditions under the new régime and decided, as Britain has been trying with the boat people in Hong Kong, to try and repatriate them by force. In the Age of the Refugees this policy, of promising handouts to a few million more, rather than enabling them to leave in dignity beforehand, was the ultimate obscenity.

Britain faces a huge crisis with Hong Kong. On behalf of its citizens there, it must persuade, threaten, cajole concessions from a truculent régime which considers itself beyond intervention from foreigners. At the same time, Britain will be trying to woo that régime on behalf of exporters in the United Kingdom, and in order to try and preserve other perceived western interests in the People's Republic.

Not, in any circumstances, an easy combination. But the initial reaction of the British government was not encouraging; it was timid and shifty. When a handful of British citizens in the Falklands were threatened with foreign oppression, this government rushed to their aid, with rousing rhetoric and clashing arms. No one could suggest a military defence of Hong Kong, but in this case even the rhetoric was missing. Dame Lydia Dunn, a member of Hong Kong's tiny Legislative Council, said, 'Why doesn't Mrs Thatcher take the high ground, and say these are British citizens whose rights must be defended?' Instead, the British reaction betrayed that same combination of reverence and terror of China that so often characterises western relations with the denizens of the Middle Kingdom today. The West's long love affair with a vision of historic China has enabled us far too often to ignore the brutality and mendaciousness of the People's Republic. We have rarely denounced Mao as we have Stalin. We make too little of the fact that for forty years the régime has murdered, imprisoned, abused and humiliated whomsoever it chooses. Circumspection, prudence, kowtowing, have been the watchwords of our behaviour. We have been afraid of their force, not confident in our strength. And that now goes for our policies towards Hong Kong.

Hong Kong consists of 400 square miles of island and a slice of the mainland of southeast China, and 5.7 million people, nearly all of them ethnic Chinese and most of them British citizens. The main island of Hong Kong rises sheer out of the sea. In recent decades, the geography of its lower slopes has constantly changed as more and more sleek skyscrapers rise along the shore and the lower slopes of the hills in every business cycle. From Hong Kong's highest point, The Peak, the islands stretch into the sea and mists to one side as in an exquisite painting on a scroll. On the other, across the glitter of the port below, the hills beyond the city lead away into the measureless depths of China. It may not be relevant to my argument, but Hong Kong is very beautiful, as well as vibrant.

Hong Kong is only fifty miles from the port of Canton or Guanzhou which, for several hundred years, has been China's link to southeast Asia and the world to the west. Portugal established its trading colony at Macao, just a few miles from Hong Kong, in the sixteenth century.

By the middle of the nineteenth century, Britain, France, America and Holland all had trading missions in Canton, but the Chinese would not allow them diplomatic relations. The chief product traded by the British was murderous opium exported from India. In 1840 the Chinese attempted to interrupt this trade, the British sent gunboats, the Chinese were forced to negotiate, and the local British Superintendent of Trade, Captain Charles Elliott, RN, demanded the rocky island of Hong Kong as a centre for British trade with China. The island, twenty-six square miles, had some 7,000 inhabitants.

Palmerston was not impressed with this deal, but the next year the Treaty of Nanking (now described by Peking as an Unequal Treaty) confirmed,

> It being obviously necessary and desirable that British subjects should have some Port whereat they may careen and refit their Ships, when required, and keep stores for that purpose, His Majesty the Emperor of China cedes to Her Majesty the Queen of Great Britain the Island of Hong Kong to be possessed in perpetuity by Her Britannic Majesty, Her Heirs and Successors and to be governed by such Laws and Regulations as Her Majesty the Queen of Great Britain shall see fit to direct.

It is said that the Emperor was filled with sadness and shame at having to cede even this tiny part of Chinese territory to the Outer Barbarians.

Twenty years later, after the Second Anglo-Chinese war, the British obtained the Kowloon peninsula, the southern tip of the mainland opposite Hong Kong island, in perpetuity. And in 1898 Britain demanded and received a ninety-nine-year lease on a much larger tract of hinterland behind Kowloon. It was this lease which decided the ultimate fate of Hong Kong.

In the first half of the twentieth century many British merchants in Hong Kong prospered, but Shanghai to the north became the most important, cosmopolitan port in China, and Hong Kong did not flourish brilliantly. It was the Chinese communist revolution which drove Shanghai into decline and made Hong Kong what it is today.

In 1945 the population of Hong Kong was some 600,000. Immediately after the 1949 revolution, hundreds of thousands of refugees began to flood in, many of them from Shanghai. By 1955 there were 2.4 million people there. Now there are nearly six million. Thus the vast majority of Hong Kong's population are either refugees or the children of refugees from communism. Since 1949 those refugees have created in Hong Kong one of the most successful city states in the history of the world – a financial and manufacturing miracle, and a capitalist wonderland. It is a crowded, rushing, hustling place, a fantastic machine for making money. The forcefulness of the economy and many of its engineers is sometimes overwhelming; many people find it hard to love Hong Kong. The British and the Chinese have never really 'met' there. Few British entrepreneurs or officials ever learned Chinese. Indeed there has been a tendency amongst some of the British to denigrate the Chinese as mere moneymakers, gamblers, main-chancers all – as if they, the whites who are there, had altogether purer interests. It is a contemptible attitude; in fact, the vast majority of Chinese who have come as refugees to Hong Kong are simply driven by the desire to master their own destinies and provide the greatest security for their families. Moreover, despite its emphasis on profiteering, Hong Kong still enjoys far more freedoms than its rival city state, Singapore, or, for that matter, anywhere else in southern Asia. There are always poor in Hong Kong; till recently they came rushing in from China. But there are always fortunes, some small, some grossly huge, to be made. The turnover in positions and wealth is fantastical and constant.

In the twelfth century, a Chinese magician poet called Bai Yeu Shan foresaw a Hong Kong blazing 'with a host of stars in the deep night, and ten thousand ships passing to and fro within the harbour'. Quoting him, the historian Jan Morris says, 'by the end of the 1980s it had all come true.'

And so it had. But all the while midnight, and the end of the spell, was approaching. Back in 1898, the one-hundred-year lease on the New Territories must have seemed an eternity away, at least to the British. (To the Chinese it was perhaps only a moment in eternity.) Through the 1960s and 1970s the clock began to spin the years, months, hours away. It was as if one could peer over the rim of the end of the day and see below only a dark and brutal future into which one would soon and inevitably fall.

By the end of the seventies, people in Hong Kong were becoming more and more worried about 1997. The British initiated talks with China on the future of the colony.

In 1979, the Governor of Hong Kong, Sir Murray Maclehose, travelled to Peking and met with Deng Xiao Ping, China's Supreme Leader then and now. After this brief but vital encounter, Maclehose reported back that Deng had said, 'Put their hearts at ease': China wanted Hong Kong's prosperity to continue. But Deng apparently also made it clear that China fully intended to regain sovereignty in 1997. No way would the lease be extended. In those few moments, it was all over.

In September 1982 Margaret Thatcher, fresh from her victory in rescuing British kith in the Falklands from Argentine oppression, visited Peking. In Hong Kong the stock market fell when Britain announced that the Prime Minister would raise the issue of Hong Kong. Many people believed it unwise to make the issue a trial of strength between the Chinese and British leaders.

But Mrs Thatcher was apparently, and understandably, anxious once again to be the Iron Lady. She took the high ground for Hong Kong and warned that as far as she was concerned the treaties were still valid. 'In conducting these talks,' she said,

'I shall speak not only for Britain, but for Britain's moral responsibility and duty to the people of Hong Kong.' But on the steps of the Great Hall of the People, Mrs Thatcher stumbled and almost fell; in Hong Kong this was seen as a very bad omen.

Her role in the talks is still shrouded. It is said that Foreign Office officials, who enjoy their exclusive understanding of Mandarin and of the workings of the Middle Kingdom, had counselled her against a confrontational approach. But it is also said that Mrs Thatcher, furious at the Foreign Office's failure to predict the invasion of the Falklands, refused to listen to such advice. It is said that she therefore talked to Deng himself of the inviolability of treaties – meaning that Hong Kong island and the Kowloon peninsula had been ceded in perpetuity to Britain – and that his response was filled with furious and untranslated expletives. These things are said, and widely. Neither Mrs Thatcher nor Mr Deng has confirmed them.

Over the next two years Britain and China held a long series of bilateral and secret talks on the future of Hong Kong. On the British side they were conducted by the small, discreet and learned troupe of sinologists in the Foreign Office.

Never were the people of Hong Kong consulted as to their wishes – Peking would not allow it – but polls showed that an overwhelming majority hoped that their return to China could be avoided. Frantic rumours about the talks seeped around and sent the Hong Kong stock market soaring or crashing, but little of substance was made known. Many in Hong Kong hoped and even believed that the British would be able to do a deal whereby the lease was extended or direct rule from Peking was in some other way delayed. But the British government abandoned Mrs Thatcher's high and risky ground. London made no attempt to argue that since Hong Kong island and the Kowloon peninsula had been ceded 'in perpetuity', they should remain British when the New Territories were handed back. Publicly the British position has been that those two areas are unviable alone and that a handover was inevitable. The only thing to be negotiated was the terms.

Undoubtedly the British tried their best to preserve what is often called 'Hong Kong's unique lifestyle' – its lack of any dogma save a dedication to the most efficient possible manufacture of money. Their principal argument with Peking was to the effect that Hong Kong was a goose most of whose golden eggs were sent to Peking. (This is indeed the truth, but China always denies it.) A central fact from which the British shied away, and which they still prefer not to discuss, was the distinction between territory and people. This seems to me absolutely crucial. There was indeed a ninety-nine-year lease on the New Territories. But there was no such lease on the people within it. They all came much later – to get away from the tyrants in Peking. Why was Britain under any obligation to return them, as well as the stones, to Peking? It was not and it is not. But the British government wished so to do. No party at Westminster wanted these people.

In September 1984, the British and Chinese governments reached an agreement, known as the Joint Declaration.

It opened thus:

1. The Government of the People's Republic of China declares that to recover the Hong Kong area (including Hong Kong Island, Kowloon and the New Territories, hereinafter referred to as Hong Kong) is the common aspiration of the entire Chinese people, and that it has decided to resume the exercise of sovereignty over Hong Kong with effect from 1 July 1997.
2. The Government of the United Kingdom declares that it will restore Hong Kong to the People's Republic of China with effect from 1 July 1997.

At least the British statement has the merit of being simple, straightforward and true. The sanctimonious Chinese reference to the 'common aspiration of the entire Chinese people' was more than usually outrageous, since several millions of that people had actually fled to the sanctuary of Hong Kong and many more millions would have liked to do so.

The agreement was widely accepted as the best

that the British government could have achieved. All of Hong Kong was to be handed back to China on 1 July 1997, but Hong Kong's 'way of life' was to be preserved for the next fifty years. The colony would become a semi-autonomous Special Administrative Region within the People's Republic. A mini-constitution known as the Basic Law was to be drawn up by China, in consultation with Hong Kong, for the governance of Hong Kong in the next fifty years. The Chinese coined the phrase, 'One country, two systems'. The other key slogans were 'Hong Kong people administering Hong Kong' and 'A high degree of autonomy'. All seem empty now, after the massacre.

The Joint Declaration was signed in Peking in December 1984 by Prime Ministers Thatcher and Zhao Xiyang, who has now been purged and accused of counter-revolution. Mrs Thatcher then stopped over in Hong Kong en route, as she took care to point out, to see President Reagan. She insisted that the agreement 'assures the continuation of Hong Kong as a free-trading capitalist society for a very long time to come – into the middle of the next century. This means that Hong Kong can plan its future with confidence. I believe Chairman Deng intends his bold concept of "One country, two systems" to last.'

It was then that Mrs Thatcher made her famous dismissal of a sceptical journalist as 'the one solitary exception' in all of Hong Kong. All the other solitary exceptions were told that no changes whatsoever could be made to the Joint Declaration. It was a fait accompli. At China's demand, the British even insisted, in the White Paper accompanying the Agreement, that 'The alternative to acceptance of the present agreement is to have no agreement'. If the people of Hong Kong rejected the work of the mandarins in Peking and the Foreign Office, they would be cast into 1997 without even this piece of paper in their hands. 'The choice is therefore between reversion of Hong Kong to China under agreed, legally binding international arrangements, or reversion to China without such arrangements.'

Over the next three years more and more people in Hong Kong came to believe that the British and Hong Kong governments were failing to protect their rights adequately. Even before the massacre, the future after 1 July 1997 was beginning to seem more and more uncertain. And so, more and more people sought to leave Hong Kong. Last year the figure was over 40,000, most of them professional people with money to buy visas or skills to sell abroad. After the massacre, foreign consulates in Hong Kong were besieged with enquiries for immigration. They ran out of forms. Tens of thousands of people who had previously been prepared to 'wait-and-see', now decided to wait no longer – they had seen enough.

$\diamondsuit$

A few weeks after the massacre I visited Hong Kong. As usual, the amount of new building, especially in the financial district, Central, astonished me. Like a gleaming unsheathed sword, the new Bank of China building, designed by the American–Chinese architect, I. M. Pei, soars over all. The clatter and the bustle were still the same, but there was about the place a smell of doom. Whiffs of Prague before 1948, as the communists sharpened their knives and prepared to whittle away the freedoms of that long democratic country. And more recent odours – from Saigon, in the months before its fall. There too everyone was talking incessantly about getting out before the communists arrived. There too young women were urgently seeking foreigners to marry to escape, while the young men looked on in anguish.

The despair engendered by the massacre was provoking some bizarre plans for mass exodus. Maybe Hong Kong could be resettled in the Western Isles. Or maybe on Guam. Perhaps in one of the more barren parts of Australia. One letter in the *South China Morning Post* even proposed the construction of a totally artificial island manufactured from some magnificent modern material. Most poignant of all perhaps was the forlorn hope that China would decide it was in its own best interests to grant another fifty-year lease.

One thing which became overwhelmingly clear right away was that the notion of 'One country, two systems' did not now have a prayer. Since the massacre, Hong Kong was inextricably tied into Chinese politics – as a centre of opposition. How could it be otherwise? Were the citizens of Hong Kong to do and say nothing about the massacre and its aftermath, its dire implications for themselves? In fact, they were speaking out – and they were being intemperately denounced from Peking for daring to do so.

Over and over, people expressed contempt for the British and the Government's stand on right of abode. 'We have sworn allegiance to the Queen,' they said. 'Maybe the land has to go back, but us?'

Over and over, I was reminded that until 1962, citizens of Hong Kong, and other parts of the Commonwealth, had the right to enter and remain in the UK freely. The Commonwealth Immigrants Act removed that right. Today several lawyers in Hong Kong are looking again at the passage of the Act to see whether it was the intention of the Act to deprive full British citizens in Hong Kong, with passports issued in London, of the right of abode.

Since 1962, the restrictions have been constantly extended. The 1981 British Nationality Act, amid widespread furore, created three different categories of citizenship, straight British, of British Dependent Territories, and Overseas Citizenship. The rules were carefully devised so as not to deny the right of entry to white colonials of British descent. Thus full citizenship was given to those with 'patrial' status, which meant having one grandparent born in Britain. British citizens of Hong Kong became citizens of British Dependent Territories with no right of abode.

Since 1981, the Act has been amended to give full citizenship to both Gibraltarians and Falklanders, even those Falklanders who had no 'patrial' connection with Britain. Some of them might, in theory, even have been Chinese.

No such kindnesses were extended to the Hong Kong Chinese. In May 1984, an official delegation from Hong Kong presented Geoffrey Howe with a manifesto demanding guarantees of the rights of British nationals in Hong Kong, including the right of passport holders to enter the UK. In Parliament, Sir Geoffrey expressed 'understanding' of 'the concerns of the British nationals in Hong Kong' and acknowledged that most of them wished to retain that nationality. But the answer was still – No.

He went on to give an early version of the excuse which by now has become a cliché. 'I do not believe that either this Parliament or a successor would favour changes which stimulated emigration from Hong Kong to the UK or elsewhere.' Never was there the slightest suggestion that the Government might use its resources to persuade Parliament to 'favour' such changes. If not vis-à-vis the UK, why not for 'elsewhere'? It's large enough. For fear of upsetting Peking.

In the secret talks, China categorically refused to consider dual nationality after 1997. Agreement was impossible and the Joint Declaration contains two parallel memoranda on the subject of nationality. Britain agreed that its citizens in Hong Kong would become Chinese, but preserved their right to carry also a (worthless) British passport. From 1 July 1997 those holding British passports in Hong Kong will be called British Nationals (Overseas); such passports will not be transmissible by descent. In the parliamentary debate which effected this change, Enoch Powell made the point that the use of the word 'British' in the new nationality status was 'calculated to deceive, will deceive and perhaps is intended to deceive'.

Powell was right. When Sir Geoffrey was asked whether these British passport-holders would have any priority over others in seeking to come to Britain, he replied, 'There is no intention to effect any change of that kind'. Thus it happened that Britain became the only country in the world to deny entry to its own nationals. What a contrast with the way in which we treated the Falklanders!

◇

Fully one hundred Hong Kong British/Chinese men fought for the freedoms of their fellow British in the Falklands. This too is remembered in Hong Kong. Seaman Chiu Man won the George Medal for conspicuous gallantry. He travelled to London to collect it. He could not stay.

One of the adjectives which is for ever associated with the Falklands war is 'paramount'. What does paramount mean? Supreme, pre-eminent, dominant, foremost, premier. What was 'paramount'? Why, the wishes of the islanders of course. Unlike those of the British Chinese in Hong Kong.

Immediately after the Argentinian invasion Mrs Thatcher began to insist that the Falklanders were British and the islands remained British territory. (So, in law, are Hong Kong island and Kowloon – but we have agreed to give them away.) In the emergency debate in the Commons she noted that the Governor of the Falklands had told her that when he left, the islanders were in tears. 'They do not want to be Argentinians.' Quite so. No more do the majority of the British Chinese wish to be citizens of the People's Republic which many of them have already fled.

Looking at the rhetoric with hindsight, it seems that it was the invasion that handed the Falklanders their apparently 'inalienable rights'. Before that act of wanton illegality by the Argentinians, the British government had been prepared to do a deal with regard to sovereignty.

In the second Falkland debate, Mrs Thatcher insisted that 'British people are to be protected wherever they may choose to live, even if they are 8,000 miles away from the House of Commons.' (Hong Kong is 7,000 miles from Westminster by air.) 'If these dictators can get away with this today, then it will be someone else's turn tomorrow.'

To the Commons, on 15 April 1982, Mrs Thatcher said, 'The people of the Falkland islands should be free to determine their own way of life and their own future. The wishes of the islanders must be paramount. What matters is what the Falkland Islanders themselves wish.'

Perhaps most relevantly, if also grandiloquently, Mrs Thatcher declared, 'We have a long and proud history of recognising the rights of others to determine their own destiny. Indeed, in that respect, we have an experience unrivalled by any other nation.' (No such right has been accorded the Hong Kong British.) 'But that right must be upheld universally and not least where it is challenged by those who are hardly conspicuous for their own devotion to democracy and liberty.' Could it be that this 'universality' ends East of Suez? The parliamentary debates on Hong Kong provided a remarkably different spectacle to those on the Falklands. 'The Iron Lady Vanishes!', and the wise monkeys of the Labour Party saw, heard and said – nothing.

In Hong Kong today, many people believe that there is another reason the UK has not wished to give usable passports. They would give people the freedom to speak out, and the UK does not want to upset China. For some journalists with no escape route, self-censorship on the subject of China may seem inevitable. After the initial outrage at Tiananmen, fears are growing. Many people who took part in the demonstrations immediately after the massacre, or who have signed petitions, are already frightened – will they be on Peking's lists in 1997?

I took the Star Ferry across the harbour and went to the Hong Kong Polytechnic to see a student who had been in Peking during the Democracy Movement. In the first draft of this pamphlet I named him. But then someone pointed out to me that this was perhaps unfair, because Peking may already be compiling lists for retribution after 1997. Maybe this is slightly paranoid, but not completely: communist régimes are notoriously and endlessly unforgiving – some of the Vietnamese boat people arriving in Hong Kong today complain that because their fathers served in the South Vietnamese régime, they cannot get education for their children. I am sure that the young man from the Poly would himself insist on standing up to be counted. But that should be his decision, not mine. I removed his name.

He led me into a dishevelled office in the students' union, and said in slow English, his palms open wide, 'Now we have democracy but all we can see ahead is darkness. Now we have the right to demonstrate but in Peking – look at 4 June. How can we depend only on the Basic Law? That's why we want the insurance policy of a right of abode elsewhere.'

Back across the harbour, I went with an interpreter to a working-class area of Hong Kong island. Older people, in their shops selling dried fish or vegetables, waved away any questions. 'There is no use for us to talk about politics . . . We do not speak English . . . We are not rich . . . We stay here . . . Perhaps we will be dead by 1997. Why bother to think about it? It's useless . . .' The younger ones all wanted to leave – but usually not for Britain; they preferred Taiwan, Singapore, Canada or the USA. 'The British government has an obligation to get us out; but if it will not, what can we do?' said Mr X, an oculist. Many people showed the inevitable ambivalence of Hong Kongers – that of being both Chinese and refugees from China. 'Hong Kong has been a British colony, so the British government has a responsibility for us,' said a woman with a street stall, Mrs Y, who

33

knew all about the Joint Declaration. 'But the rich people should stay here and help construct Hong Kong. The British government must make China keep its promise on the fifty years of Hong Kong lifestyle.' A young man, Z, serving in a dry-cleaning shop, said that since 4 June, 'the future is not bright. The British have earned a lot from Hong Kong, so they have an obligation to us. Right of abode is a must – for insurance; but I would stay here unless the situation became desperate. This is my home. If the Chinese did here as in Tiananmen, then I would want to leave.'

In Central, I went into one of the most expensive office buildings in the world, Exchange Square, which was recently built on land reclaimed from the harbour. There a financier, Sin-ming Shaw, who has an American passport, was eloquent in his contempt for the British.

Britain may have taken care of its legal responsibilities, he said, 'But what about the moral ones?' Shaw thought that the way Britain was now 'dumping' the people would make them more and more panicked and embittered. Hong Kong would become ungovernable. He thought Britain now must build all possible safeguards against misrule by Peking in 1997, even if these seemed as fragile as 'panes of glass'.

He had with him a friend from Peking, an intellectual from a think tank linked to the now disgraced 'liberal' prime minister Zhao Xiyang. He was on the brink of becoming a permanent exile. He looked quite shattered by recent events; speaking fast, he was pessimistic about China, which he called a corrupt feudal dictatorship. He thought the leadership would not soon change. Its powerbase, among the army and corrupt officials, including those doing business in Hong Kong, was too strong. 'Don't forget,' someone else said to me, 'from Stalin to Gorbachev took thirty-three years.'

Shaw spoke of the 'collaborationists' in Hong Kong. Some are mega-rich men who are building new fortunes in China and want nothing to disturb the process – above all no democracy in Hong Kong. An executive system – such as exists now – completely biddable to Peking was fine with them. Indeed, the British position during the negotiations with Peking was somewhat undercut by the parade of Hong Kong fat cats preening themselves in Peking, happily believing and doing everything Peking mellifluously told them. When I was in Hong Kong, some of these same people, and their British counterparts, were contemplating a massive public relations campaign against the British Government on the right of abode. But they backed away and reverted to their own weasel word, 'pragmatism'. They, of course, will have golden parachutes in 1997.

But most 'collaborationists', like most others, have

no parachutes, nor even dinghies. They are the people who simply argue that China is so vast and terrifying, and Hong Kong's defences so slight, that Hong Kong people must be as respectful as possible.

Shaw expatiated on the continued, amazing production of money in Hong Kong and pointed out how closely intertwined it is now with the neighbouring mainland province of Guangdong; Hong Kong businesses have invested about two billion dollars and employ some two million people there. Hong Kong now earns over sixty per cent of China's foreign exchange. But if the vicious new orthodoxies in Peking force the Chinese economy into recession, dragging Hong Kong down with it, 'then Hong Kong will become like Casablanca', with visas being the only currency. Already the issue of who has and who has not a means of escape is divisive, and is creating a horrible new form of class system.

Looking out over the panorama of the harbour, Shaw was scathing about the British government's attitude on right of abode. 'If they are so confident that all will be OK, what do they have to fear? No one will leave in that case.'

Let us look at the paradox. If Hong Kong is to continue to function, then people must have hope for their own future. After the massacre, that hope can no longer be vested in Peking. If they are not given at least an ultimate right of abode in Britain now, then they will seek it elsewhere. Already the turnover in middle management jobs in Hong Kong is fantastic, something like sixty per cent, as more and more people leave. The *South China Morning Post* is one of the most profitable papers in the world because of its Jobs Vacant columns. When I was there two stories amongst dozens were big news. The French government was giving 100 passports to employees of French banks. And more than 100 top aircraft mechanics were leaving Hong Kong's airline, Cathay Pacific, to work for Qantas – because they had been promised Australian passports.

Just what are the figures? There are about 5.7 million people in Hong Kong now. At least 3.28 million residents of Hong Kong have or could now have British Dependent Territories passports. The others can or will hold Certificates of Identity. After seven years' residence in Hong Kong all Certificate holders are entitled to apply for these diminished British passports.

The Foreign Office argument is that if the right of abode were granted then Britain would have to plan on the basis that all 3.28 million presently entitled to come would do so. But this is simply a clever way of saying that Britain can obviously do no such thing. The only conceivable situation in which three million might seek to leave Hong Kong is one of absolute emergency – such as a military invasion or an explosion at the Daya Bay nuclear

37

station which China is building (to the terror of some and the profit of others) a few miles down the coast. In any such emergency an international rescue mission would have to be mounted and nationality issues would be irrelevant.

But if not three million, how many might come to Britain, if they were given the right of abode? This is almost impossible to measure, and depends on developments in China. But if they are given the security of ultimate right of abode, the overwhelming majority would wish to stay in Hong Kong unless conditions there become quite intolerable: they can make far better lives there than anywhere else. A recent poll showed that only six per cent of people in Hong Kong would wish to live in Britain.

However, without such insurance, more and more people will seek to make alternative arrangements. Canada is a favoured destination and in fact the experience of Vancouver, where about 5,000 Hong Kong Chinese have been settling every year, shows that they have been of overwhelming economic benefit. After 4 June, the Canadian High Commission received 30,000 enquiries. There is little doubt that after the massacre the number of emigrés next year will rise as high as the quotas set by the recipient countries. That will probably mean around 160,000 over the next two years.

These will come largely from the professional and managerial sections of the population – and that is a sector of about 900,000 people at most. Such a level of emigration will have a catastrophic effect on businesses in Hong Kong. I was frequently reminded that Article 4 of the Joint Declaration states that Britain will hand over Hong Kong as a going concern. Unless Britain does all it can to preserve people's confidence in staying, that will be impossible.

In the mid-eighties, British officials used to say that China would never tolerate Britain giving massive numbers of passports; they claimed it would contravene at least the spirit of the Joint Declaration and would suggest that Britain had no faith in it. That may well have been true.

However, Chinese officials have since said that it is entirely a British decision. Last year Portugal announced that it would give passports to all its some 300,000 citizens in Macao, which reverts to China in 1999 – yet Britain refuses to do the same. Portugal has been infinitely more generous to the citizens of its former empire. All were offered abode – and about one million accepted. That's in a country of only six million. After 1992, the Macao Chinese will have the right to come to Britain, via Portugal. Two hundred million other Europeans will also have the right to live in Britain. But the British citizens of Hong Kong will not. This is unforgivable.

It is also, I would argue, stupid. A study by

London University economists, led by Professor Bernard Corry, was recently commissioned and published by the *South China Morning Post*. This shows that although the influx of 3.28 million people would indeed cause serious strains on housing, transport and the unskilled labour market in Britain, it would also produce substantial benefits – to the balance of payments, to Britain's capital account, and to the 'dependency ratio' of those of working age to children and the elderly. Altogether it concluded that the benefits would outweigh the costs. Has the Government ever proposed such an analysis? Never. Nor, scandalously, has the Labour Party. (One wonders whether Labour's reluctance to allow Hong Kong Chinese into Britain has anything to do with the fact that they would probably vote Tory.)

While I was in Hong Kong, Sir Geoffrey ambled through on a whistlestop visit; his performance was depressing. He found the anger and disappointment intense. Even the Governor of Hong Kong, Sir David Wilson, was now demanding the right of abode for 3.28 million people. Demonstrators abused Sir Geoffrey at a public lunch. But he made it clear that he had no time for other views. He told protesters who visited him at Government House that they had only two minutes to present their case. At a press conference he dismissed diligent questioners as 'hecklers' and talked again of 'flexibility'. He promised 'early announcement' of a 'scheme that will make some provision for people' who have been of service to Hong Kong. How would these lucky few be selected, he was asked, and would the list be published like the New Year's Honours? Instead of an OBE, a means of escape? Yet again, Sir Geoffrey brandished 'parliamentary opposition' to making any large-scale concessions on right of abode. But he nonetheless had the audacity to admit, in a television interview, that if he were a Hong Kong Chinese, he too would be looking for the exit.

In October 1986, two years after the Joint Agreement was revealed, a somewhat different visit took place. The Queen came to Hong Kong. She told her subjects, 'You have been promised in that agreement that the institutions, traditions, and way of life so important to the people of Hong Kong will be preserved. . . . As you move towards a new phase in your development, our thoughts will always be with you.' Over the next three years, Her Majesty must have become increasingly alarmed for the future of the inhabitants of one of the last parts of her empire.

It was inevitable that the influence of China over Hong Kong would increase in that time. But few expected the extent to which that has happened. And even fewer foresaw that the British and Hong Kong governments would do so little to try and resist it. In the words of Martin Lee, QC, one of the Government's fiercest critics, 'They kowtowed.'

I went to see Mr Lee, a slim, precise man who has emerged as the most effective if unofficial 'leader of the opposition' in Hong Kong. He considers recent British weakness lamentable. 'Every time you allow the Chinese to bully you, you make it ten times more difficult for us not to be bullied after 1997.' He thinks that Britain had hoped that the Hong Kong problem would disappear with the signing of the Joint Declaration. But it did not, and now Hong Kong is 'in rebellion' against Peking. He argues that the spirit of the Joint Declaration can only survive with a package – right of abode, a properly guaranteed bill of rights, democracy, the PLA – which is now known in Hong Kong as the 'People's Liquidation Army' – to remain outside of Hong Kong, a greater degree of autonomy, and United Nations monitoring that human rights are being preserved after 1997. But now is the time to fight. 'The British government can only avert disaster by taking a strong line against China. In the last four years they have been much too weak.'

Those years have been dominated by the issue of direct elections and discussion over the development of the Basic Law, which is due to be promulgated in 1990. Many people in Hong Kong came to believe that the British and Hong Kong governments were not prepared to fight hard enough on behalf of the interests of Hong Kong. (Equally, I think Hong Kong has done too little on its own behalf.) Indeed, Britain was so terrified at giving any offence to China, that the Government made no effective protest at Chinese brutality in Tibet in 1987 and even refused to let the Dalai Lama visit Britain unless he promised not to criticise Peking. It was not lost on the people of Hong Kong that Tibet had also been promised autonomy by China.

The Joint Declaration stated that Britain 'will be responsible for the administration of Hong Kong' until 1997. But Peking has frequently criticised the British for allegedly deviating from the Declaration. The British and the Hong Kong governments have often failed to respond robustly, arguing that they should not upset Peking and jeopardise Sino-British relations.

Nowhere has this been more true than in the matter of elections. Unlike in its other colonies, Britain has never allowed the development of democratic institutions in Hong Kong. China's disapproval has always been cited – at least since 1949. The best that can be said for this is that Britain gave Hong Kong a dictatorship which was benign. We are turning it over to one which is murderous.

The Governor of Hong Kong is in fact its Viceroy. He takes advice from a Legislative Council of fifty-six appointed members and members indirectly elected through associations. Before the Joint Declaration, Britain frequently said that it would allow the direct election of a few members of the Legislative Council for the first time in 1988 and that by 1997 a substantial number of these councillors would be directly elected. The Declaration itself allowed for elections, but fudged the issue: it did not specifically state that these should be direct elections. To begin with, all looked well. Richard Luce, then Minister of State for Hong Kong, said in the House of Commons debate on the Joint Declaration, 'We all fully accept that we should build up a firmly based democratic administration in Hong Kong in the years between now and 1997.'

But after the Joint Declaration was signed, and in defiance of Britain's sole responsibility, Chinese officials constantly complained about any such extension of the franchise. One key incident, often cited, was at the end of 1985 when the head of the Xinhua News Agency in Hong Kong, in effect China's Shadow Governor, gave a press conference, tapped his spectacles on the table and warned, 'Someone is departing from the Joint Declaration.' He was talking about direct elections and his warning had an effect. Neither the British nor the Hong Kong governments protested publicly.

44

Instead, British ministers found another weasel word – 'convergence'. There must be 'convergence' between political development in Hong Kong and the provisions of the Basic Law. Convergence was a euphemism for watering down existing rights in Hong Kong to fit China's vision of the future.

In January 1986, Timothy Renton, the Foreign Office minister with responsibility for Hong Kong, visited Peking and said that, without convergence, 'there obviously could be a very unpleasant jolt some time after 1997'. That is absolutely not the point; on the contrary the British should have been anxious to create whatever safeguards they can against Chinese dictatorship. Democracy delayed is democracy denied.

In 1987 Deng Xiao Ping impatiently dismissed democracy as 'all that Western stuff'. In November 1987 Thatcher and Howe refused to meet with a delegation demanding early direct elections. The Hong Kong government then produced a survey purporting to show that the people of Hong Kong were divided on whether they wanted early direct elections or not. (Many people dismissed the figures as cooked or absurd; other surveys showed a large majority in favour of direct elections.) The 1988 White Paper on elections was very different from that published in 1984. The 1984 White Paper had found that 'with few exceptions' the people of Hong Kong wished to vote for some of their legislators in 1988 and for 'a significant number' by 1997. But in 1988, the Government claimed that the people of Hong Kong were 'sharply divided' on the issue, and so deferred it until 1991. Sir Geoffrey now claimed that direct elections in 1988 had never been promised and that the Government's approach was 'evolutionary rather than revolutionary'. In other words it had evolved to accept China's opposition to elections. Despite all the British pledges, direct elections in 1988 were dropped. Thus political representation in Hong Kong is still in its infancy.

Peking has shown far fewer scruples and has actively encouraged the work of the Chinese Communist Party in Hong Kong. Since 1985, Xinhua, China's 'Ministry of Truth', has opened three new offices in different areas of Hong Kong; their staffs have assiduously set themselves up as alternatives to the government district offices. (There is a bitter but good joke about Xinhua. Deng Xiao Ping meets Napoleon – in Hell, I presume – and Deng says, 'If I had had your cavalry, I would have won the battle of Tiananmen.' Napoleon replies, 'If I'd had your Xinhua, no one would have known that I'd lost the battle of Waterloo.') Some democratic activists in Hong Kong have warned that the Communists' new organisation raises fundamental questions about Peking's real commitment to Hong Kong's autonomy. The director of Xinhua has said that after 1997, the role of the Chinese Communist Party will be 'to assist the SAR (Special Administrative Region) Government.'

All of this reminds me of the way in which Hungarian and Czechoslovak Stalinists began to organise the subversion of democracy in their countries between 1945 and 1948. They sliced little by little at the existing freedoms and democratic institutions. Salami tactics, it was called.

Just as crucial as the right to choose their representatives, will be the Basic Law – the constitution which will govern the people of Hong Kong from 1997. On this question also, China seems to have much more definite and aggressive views than does Britain.

In her 1984 press conference in Hong Kong, Mrs Thatcher said that Deng Xiao Ping had told her that China would solicit the view of Hong Kong 'on a wide basis up until 1990' in the drafting of the Basic Law. That has not proved to be the case. The consultations between Hong Kong and Peking over the Basic Law to date give little reason for confidence. No genuine dialogue between local lawyers and Chinese lawyers on the drafting committee has ever really been established. When lawyers from Peking visited the Supreme Court in

47

Hong Kong during the handover talks, they seemed astonished to learn that individual citizens won cases against the Government. In China, by contrast, lawyers tend to join the judges in abusing their own trembling clients. In China, the accused are presumed guilty, not innocent. They have no protection, and appeals are always a formality. Those sentenced to death are frequently humiliated before being shot in the back of the head with a bullet for which their relatives have to pay. Now there are reports of secret executions of Democracy activists.

The first draft of the Basic Law was published in 1988 and was widely criticised in Hong Kong as offering inadequate guarantees to the people of Hong Kong.

One fundamental problem is that there is no formal recognition within the Chinese Constitution that a region may have a system, like that of Hong Kong, which completely contradicts the spirit as well as the letter of the People's Republic.

Article 31 of the Constitution allows the creation of such Special Regions as Tibet and Hong Kong. But Article 5 provides that no law shall be passed which contravenes the Constitution. Yet the Basic Law is supposed to protect capitalism in Hong Kong. So does Article 31 override Article 5? Nowhere in the Constitution is that stated. It surely follows that there is at the least an inconsistency in the Constitution, and one which a government in Peking could, if it so wished, exploit. Indeed papers put out by the mainland drafters of the Basic Law have stated precisely that 'The Constitution shall on the whole be applicable to Hong Kong.'

Within the general contextual problem, there are other specific concerns. For example, Articles 25 and 49 of the Chinese Constitution promote family planning – which has meant female infanticide, tragically committed by parents desperate that their one permitted child should be a boy; Article 37 of the Draft Basic Law allows the people of Hong Kong 'the right to raise a family'. Article 36 of the Chinese Constitution discriminates against Catholics maintaining union with Rome; the Basic Law allows Hong Kong Catholics to do so.

Such inconsistencies may seem quibbles, but they tend to raise doubts as to how securely founded the Hong Kong Region will be within China.

Consider one more and very crucial matter. Who has the final right of interpretation of the law? Remember, in China justice is revolutionary justice.

Under Article 67 of the Chinese Constitution, the Standing Committee of the National People's Congress has such power. Article 157 of the Draft Basic Law extends this power to Hong Kong. This is appalling. It completely undermines the existing common law system, the independence of the judiciary and the final right of adjudication. Moreover, the Standing Committee is given the right to decide which of Hong Kong's present laws are consistent with the Basic Law and which have to be changed. There is no provision for the people of Hong Kong to have any say in such decisions.

Sir Geoffrey, in evidence to the House Foreign Affairs Committee, tried to downplay the importance of Article 157, saying that its role was similar to that of the European Court vis-à-vis Britain. But the Court is a judicial body; the Congress is a legislative or political one, and its Standing Committee is charged with enforcing the Constitution. These are crucial and disturbing differences. It is essential that Hong Kong courts have the power to decide whether Hong Kong legislation abides by the Basic Law. Once that power is given to apparatchiks in Peking, Hong Kong is lost.

Before the massacre, the apparent weakness of the British and Hong Kong governments in face of obduracy and bullying from Peking had already led to a massive loss of confidence in Hong Kong. Tiananmen did not alter the nature of the communist government of China. But it revealed it in all its spasmodic, dying brutality. The massacre and its aftermath have created a completely new situation; previous British policies were already shamefully inadequate. Now they are totally indefensible. As this pamphlet goes to press, the Chinese are appearing characteristically thuggish and blustering. With harsh vulgarity, they are denouncing their critics in Hong Kong; they have singled out Martin Lee for attack; they are insisting on the right to station the PLA in Hong Kong in 1997; they are threatening all and sundry. As a result, despair is spreading like cancer. The new Foreign Secretary, John Major, must act radically.

In the best of all possible worlds, Peking would be persuaded that it is in its own interest to extend the lease on Hong Kong for another fifty years. That seems unlikely to happen. The Joint Declaration should not be torn up – that might well produce a worse crisis of confidence than that which now exists. But the Chinese must be kept diligently to it; the British must not weakly allow them to reinterpret it. One analogy made by Martin Lee is that of a foster parent handing a child back to its natural parent. What if, after the agreement is made, the natural parent turns out to be a killer? Does the child still have to go back?

After the massacre, Britain is in a strong bargaining position vis-à-vis Peking, which has been internationally humiliated (and impoverished) by its own brutality. More protection for Hong Kong must be negotiated. Hong Kong must indeed retain 'a high degree of autonomy' and be run by local inhabitants.

Otherwise, London can say, it will be impossible to hand back Hong Kong as a stable and prosperous society as the Joint Declaration requires.

Here are some of the responsibilities that Britain must now undertake to honour its commitments to Hong Kong. This is neither an exhaustive nor a detailed list.

1.   The right of escape is paramount. The people of Hong Kong are either British citizens or under British protection. They must not simply be forcibly repatriated to a régime which can perpetrate such outrages as Tiananmen. Britain must give right of abode. This must be done in the context of an international resettlement scheme. London should even now be taking the lead in persuading the Commonwealth, the EEC and other governments with a stake in Hong Kong, notably the USA, to devise a massive resettlement scheme for those who do not wish to be cast back into China. Many will have to be given rights of abode in Britain. This will cause serious problems, of course. But it is almost impossible that the numbers would be as high as the Foreign Office claims. The Government and the Labour party must cease their eager and revolting obeisance to the spectre of British racism.

The granting of widespread right of abode will have several effects. First it will reassure all those in Hong Kong who are understandably frightened of having their children grow up under Peking's fist. The overwhelming majority will stay unless conditions become intolerable. Second, it will make Britain much more committed to seeing that all does go well in Hong Kong – for then people will not wish to come to Britain, to the relief of the British government. Third, it will give the people of Hong Kong the liberty to express their views without fear of retaliation after 1997. Fourth, and for all the above reasons, it will make the Chinese more careful of Hong Kong. Indeed that will be the most powerful and important effect of the right of abode. It will put the moral and practical responsibility squarely on China to create decent conditions, from which the people of Hong Kong will not want to flee.

2.   For Hong Kong to be able to bargain effectively with China it *must* have leaders freely elected by the community. That too is paramount. Direct elections to the Legislative Council must be instituted before 1997. Certainly twenty members could be elected in 1991 and all by 1995. How else can a local leadership emerge which is answerable to the Hong Kong people? If the Chinese object, let them dismantle the system after they take charge. Perhaps elections and other safeguards are merely 'panes of glass'. But they must be installed anyway; glass usually makes effective shields. Let the Chinese

53

government bear the odium if it wishes to smash them later.

3. A Bill of Rights must be incorporated in the Basic Law, even though this might merely be another 'pane of glass'.

4. Britain must persuade China that the Basic Law, as drafted, does not represent the spirit of the Joint Declaration – and does not promote China's own interests. It must push China to make substantial improvements. It should insist that the People's Liberation Army not be stationed in Hong Kong. (They can get there very fast by train anyway.) The Joint Declaration merely says that Peking 'may' station troops. It would be an important gesture for Peking to waive this right. Furthermore, the Governor of Hong Kong, not Peking, should have the power to declare martial law.

At the same time there are urgent actions required by Hong Kong itself. The community is very badly represented abroad; it needs much more competent and visible envoys to argue its case on television and to government in London and other major capitals. There are immense resources in Hong Kong; they should be deployed. At the same time the people of Hong Kong should be showing a good deal more generosity of spirit to the Vietnamese boat people who arrive there – they are fleeing just the sort of régime Hong Kong wishes to avoid. Why should the world show sympathy for Hong Kong's citizens if they show none for the Vietnamese?

The Government of Hong Kong must now try to separate itself from London. It must be seen to represent the people of Hong Kong not the prejudices of British voters. This is beginning to happen. I attended a debate in the traditionally panelled chamber of the Legislative Assembly in which speaker after speaker excoriated the British government for its failure to grant abode. The Government Secretary, Sir David Ford, joined the criticism. This was unprecedented – and overdue. Since the massacre, Sir David Wilson has spoken out more forcefully on behalf of right of abode and other issues than before. He needs to. He is no longer merely a gifted sinologist, academic and diplomat. The last British Governor of Hong Kong is the most important Viceroy since Mountbatten. He stands for almost six million people.

The bottom line is this. Britain has agreed to turn the people of Hong Kong over to a defunct and cruel dictatorship. It used to be argued that the British government had no alternative. More important is the fact that in the last five years the British and Hong Kong governments have done too little to safeguard the future of the people. After the massacre, far more effective safeguards and

55

real rights of escape are essential. Otherwise the betrayal of British subjects in Hong Kong will be far more significant in the history of the Thatcher government than the rescue of other subjects in the Falklands. It will be a deed of craven baseness.

◇

I went on a launch of the Royal Hong Kong police, to an island where some 2,000 Vietnamese boat people were camping on the hillsides in filthy conditions. Fourteen years after the end of the Vietnam war, they are still haemorrhaging out of their country, complaining of the hateful nature of the régime. In the South China Sea, they risk rape and brutal murder from Thai pirates. Hitherto they have been accepted but incarcerated in Hong Kong; there are now 45,000 there. The way they are now being treated is unconscionable. While I was in the colony the British government was trying to negotiate their forcible repatriation to Vietnam – a deal which Washington denounced as 'odious' and which has now been suspended.

So I should hope. Forced repatriation would be an intolerable, unforgivable assault on people who are merely trying to escape dictatorship. That is at last becoming possible in many places, as barbed wire is cut down. As I correct these final paragraphs,

Hungary has refused to force thousands of East Germans back into the clutches of its own ally; overjoyed, they are pouring into the West. It is grotesque that at such a time Britain should even consider the forced repatriation of the Vietnamese; their motives are very similar to those of the East Germans. But could it be that London actually wishes to create a precedent? This dreadful thought occurs because, after all, forced repatriation is exactly what Britain is planning for its own citizens in 1997.

As we slid out of Aberdeen harbour in Hong Kong, the boat people's fragile, unpainted sailing junks, roped together under the Yacht Club, looked like broken eggshells or crumpled leaves. All around them were the gleaming, varnished motor junks of the Chinese middle classes.

Like almost all other refugees in the world today, the Vietnamese are fleeing a man-made disaster. Hong Kong could easily become another. But that is not inevitable. It is the absolute responsibilty of the British government not to kowtow. It must work without cease to ensure that all the lustrous weekend junks in Aberdeen harbour are not themselves soon being washed up on other Asian shores, crammed with British refugees, waving British passports stamped – DISHONOURED.

CHATTO
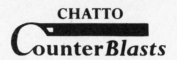
Counter*Blasts*

Also available in bookshops now:-

Forthcoming Chatto Counter*Blasts*:

Counter*Blasts* to be published in 1990 include:-

Tessa Blackstone on prisons and penal reform

Douglas Dunn on Poll Tax

Ludovic Kennedy on euthanasia

Adam Mars-Jones on Venus Envy

Adam Lively on sovereignty

Margaret Drabble on property and mortgage tax relief

Ronald Dworkin on a Bill of Rights for Britain

Plus pamphlets from Michael Holroyd, Harold Evans, Hanif Kureishi, Michael Ignatieff, Edward Mortimer and Susannah Clapp

If you want to join in the debate, and if you want to know more about **Counter*Blasts***, the writers and the issues, then write to:

Random House UK Ltd, Freepost 5066, Dept MH, London WC1B 3BR